To my parents, John and Rosemary Lyon, who are curious and engaged in the world—just like Ruth
—J. L.

To my grandparents, for all your love and support
—A. B.

MARGARET K. McELDERRY BOOKS
An imprint of Simon & Schuster Children's Publishing Division
1230 Avenue of the Americas, New York, New York 10020
Text copyright © 2021 by Julia Lyon
Illustrations copyright © 2021 by Alexandra Bye
Book design © 2021 by Simon & Schuster, Inc.
All rights reserved, including the right of reproduction in whole or in part in any form.
MARGARET K. McELDERRY BOOKS is a trademark of Simon & Schuster, Inc.
For information about special discounts for bulk purchases, please contact Simon & Schuster
Special Sales at 1-866-506-1949 or business@simonandschuster.com.
The Simon & Schuster Speakers Bureau can bring authors to your live event. For more
information or to book an event, contact the Simon & Schuster Speakers Bureau at
1-866-248-3049 or visit our website at www.simonspeakers.com.
The text for this book was set in Dante MT.
The illustrations for this book were rendered digitally.
Manufactured in China
0721 SCP
First Edition
2 4 6 8 10 9 7 5 3 1
Library of Congress Cataloging-in-Publication Data
Names: Lyon, Julia, author. | Bye, Alexandra, illustrator.
Title: A dinosaur named Ruth : how Ruth Mason discovered fossils in her own backyard /
written by Julia Lyon ; illustrated by Alexandra Bye.
Description: First edition. | New York : Margaret K. McElderry Books, 2021. | Includes
bibliographical references. | Audience: Ages 4–8 | Audience: Grades K–1 | Summary: "When
prairie girl Ruth Mason finds strange rocks on her family land, she devotes her life to uncovering
their source, leading to the discovery of thousands of dinosaur fossils"—Provided by publisher.
Identifiers: LCCN 2021007000 (print) | LCCN 2021007001 (ebook) |
ISBN 9781534474642 (hardcover) | ISBN 9781534474635 (ebook)
Subjects: LCSH: Mason, Ruth, 1898?–1990—Juvenile literature. | Dinosaurs—South Dakota—Juvenile literature. |
Ranchers—South Dakota—Biography—Juvenile literature. | Edmontosaurus—South Dakota—Juvenile literature.
Classification: LCC QE861.8.S8 L96 2021 (print) | LCC QE861.8.S8 (ebook) | DDC 567.9—dc23
LC record available at https://lccn.loc.gov/2021007000
LC ebook record available at https://lccn.loc.gov/2021007001

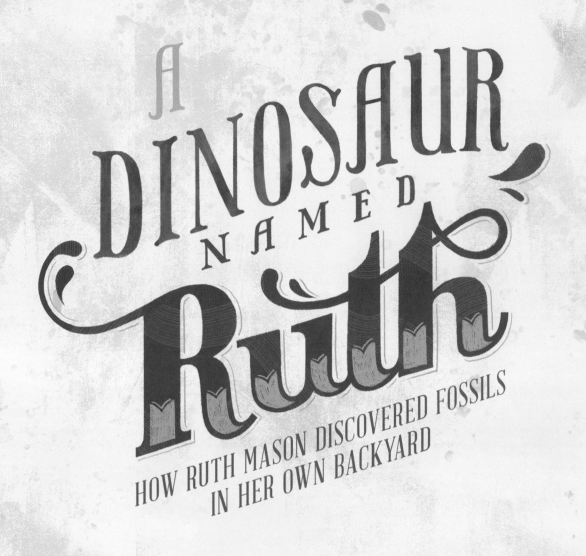

A DINOSAUR NAMED Ruth

HOW RUTH MASON DISCOVERED FOSSILS IN HER OWN BACKYARD

Written by

Julia Lyon

Illustrated by

Alexandra Bye

Margaret K. McElderry Books
New York   London   Toronto   Sydney   New Delhi

Ruth Mason was forever curious about her own backyard.
Its secrets. Its stories. Its quiet clues.

She was a girl who kept asking questions—and never stopped—
until she revealed the mystery beneath her busy feet.

Millions of years ago, a tropical forest covered
this western land near the edge of a great sea.
Dinosaurs thundered across the shore.

Millions of years later, here was Ruth: climbing
trees and riding stick horses into the sunset.

It was 1905. The grassy prairie was her playground, spilling out around her family's log cabin, in the new state of South Dakota.

She didn't know that a very old world lay close enough to touch.

She didn't know that dinosaurs once lived
in her own backyard.

Then one day—when she was seven—
Ruth found them.

Clues!

She picked up these small pieces of the past, cradled them in her hand, and tucked them in her apron pocket.

At home, no one could answer her questions. No one thought much of the strange rubble she found on the ground.

So the dinosaur experts didn't race toward her family's ranch. The museums didn't come to investigate.

But Ruth wondered. And wondered. About animals, about bones, about anything that might explain this puzzle poking out of the hills of the Badlands.

She kept collecting. Soon, she had the first seeds for her garden of bones.

As Ruth grew up, she never gave up on her backyard mystery. She wrote letters to experts at museums and universities. One after another told Ruth her finds were worthless. Not important. Nothing special.

Ruth didn't believe them. She knew enough about the land to know that what she kept finding wasn't ordinary. It was—perhaps—even extraordinary.

After each new discovery in the hills near her home, Ruth
laid her finds out in the summer sun. As the decades passed,
her collection grew under her elm trees. A collection of
ancient secrets harvested from her land. Some bones were
so large, she left them sitting out in the pasture.

She kept collecting, and her garden bloomed.

Every day, Ruth woke up early to
feed the horses, sheep, and cows.

She kept licking her envelopes and stamps,
putting her faith and questions in the
mail. All she needed was one person to
drive down the long, dusty road to see her
treasures. The answer came back in the
mail: not important, nothing special.

Dear Professor,

Ruth

Then, finally, when she was about eighty
years old, someone knocked on her door.

A fossil hunter named Rick Brooks stood on her doorstep. He was looking for remains of sea creatures that once lived in the ancient waters nearby. She didn't have what he was looking for, but Ruth invited him to see her collection in the yard.

They stepped outside into Ruth's radiant garden.

Bones surrounded every tree, sprinkled
among the flowers and neatly trimmed grass,
arranged as carefully as an artist's canvas.

Ruth's treasures were definitely fossil
bones, he told her, millions of years old.
He promised to help.

Ruth smiled wide.

It was 1979. Dinosaur experts arrived at Ruth's ranch. Bones—including pieces of jaws and teeth—jutted out of the steep banks of the Badlands. The experts were astounded. After slowly removing layers of earth, they found thousands of bones, representing at least ninety-nine dinosaurs.

Ruth was right. Her finds *were* important. They were extraordinary indeed.

Ruth welcomed back the ancient neighbors she had wondered about for so long.

Her quiet ranch transformed. Bone hunters, paleontologists, dinosaur dreamers, and students spent years harvesting the earth. They were the collectors now, revealing thousands of duck-billed dinosaur bones, fragments of *Triceratops* bones, *Tyrannosaurus rex* teeth, and the jaws of ancient marsupials whose story could now be told.

Ruth soaked up the history of the land, even as her time on the ranch was coming to an end.

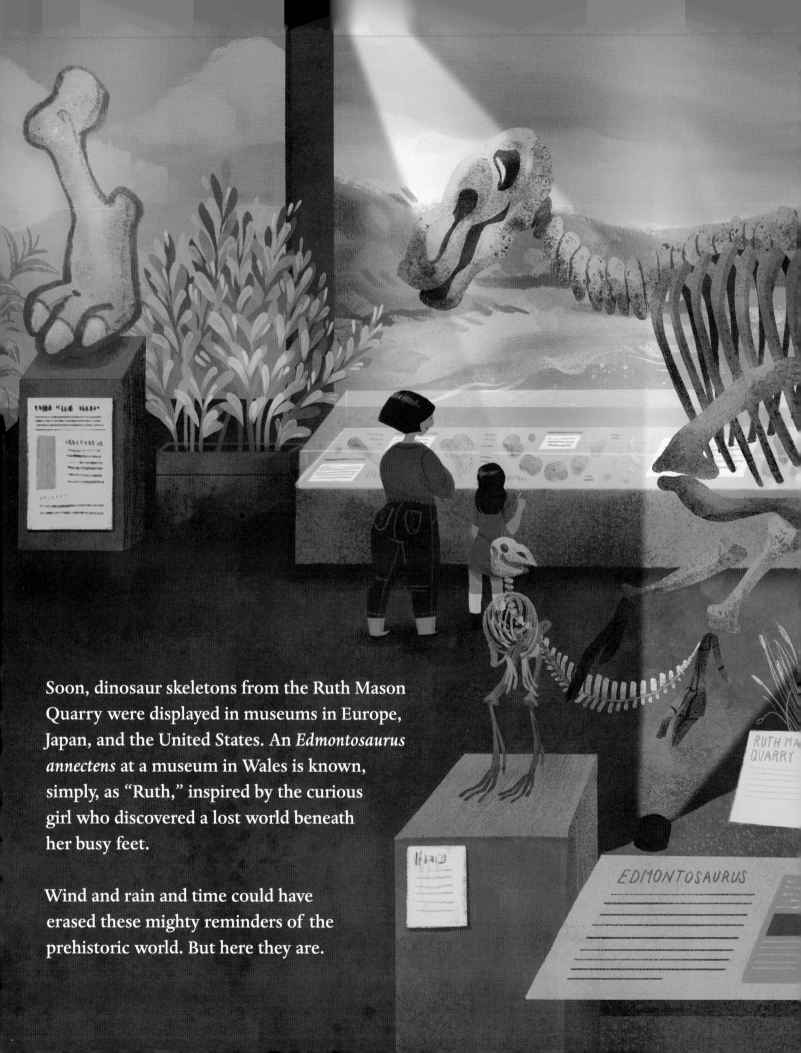

Soon, dinosaur skeletons from the Ruth Mason Quarry were displayed in museums in Europe, Japan, and the United States. An *Edmontosaurus annectens* at a museum in Wales is known, simply, as "Ruth," inspired by the curious girl who discovered a lost world beneath her busy feet.

Wind and rain and time could have erased these mighty reminders of the prehistoric world. But here they are.

RUTH MA
QUARRY

EDMONTOSAURUS

Thanks to one very patient girl named Ruth who pulled the past from her pocket and showed it to the world.

AUTHOR'S NOTE

This book is based on the true story of Ruth Mason. She found dinosaur fossil bones on her family's ranch as a child growing up in pioneer-era South Dakota. Although the details of her initial discovery can only be imagined, she did indeed collect prehistoric treasures at a young age and pursued answers until her final years.

Ruth's family was among the first pioneers to settle in the area around Faith, South Dakota, where they raised horses and, later, cattle. She was born in 1898, when the state was truly "young." South Dakota became a state in 1889. Ruth is said to have watched with classmates as workers laid the cornerstone of the state capitol building in Pierre, the city she lived in during some of her childhood.

It was very different back then. At a time when just getting to a school could require several days of travel, as it did in Ruth's earliest years, gathering information about the prehistoric past or even asking a teacher about dinosaurs would have been challenging. Books were hard to access; libraries were far away.

Dinosaurs had been found in the American West, but Ruth certainly wasn't a dinosaur expert. No one recalls her having a collection of books on dinosaurs. They do recall her curiosity and scientific mind.

In the 1960s, the discovery of *Deinonychus* fossils in nearby Montana might have piqued Ruth's interest. At some point, she contacted the South Dakota School of Mines & Technology and other experts about the fossils on her ranch.

Rick Brooks met Ruth while visiting landowners during a fossil-scouting expedition. About a year later, he introduced Ruth to Pete Larson, a founder of the Black Hills Institute of Geological Research.

"The best thing that came of that for me was that I was able to help that woman see her dream come true," Brooks said.

Black Hills Institute excavated Ruth's land from 1979 to 1991. Their work resulted in ten mounted dinosaur skeletons displayed across the world, as well as many "touch bones." Those are typically femur bones that children are allowed to touch, now located in museums in Europe, Japan, Canada, and the United States.

Ruth's quarry inspired both landowners and dinosaur hunters to look for more fossils in the region. In 1990, Sue Hendrickson discovered "Sue," a massive *Tyrannosaurus rex*, on land nearby.

Today, Ruth's grandniece owns the ranch. She, too, collects bones from the land. A *Triceratops* horn sits in her front yard. A piece of *Ankylosaurus* armor rests in her living room. The tooth of a *Tyrannosaurus rex* perches near the sofa.

What Is an *Edmontosaurus annectens*?

A duck-billed dinosaur, this creature was an herbivore that lived during the Late Cretaceous Period, which ended about sixty-six million years ago. *Edmontosaurus annectens* could have more than one thousand teeth and usually stretched about thirty-five feet from head to tail.

The dinosaur known as "Ruth" has been housed at the National Museum Cardiff in Wales for more than twenty-five years. This

Ruth came to Wales because the museum
wanted to feature a dinosaur to bring in
visitors. It's rare to find dinosaur fossils in Wales.

Black Hills Institute told the National Museum
that it had named the dinosaur Ruth after the quarry
owner, and so the informal name remained.

Kids Dig at the Ruth Mason Quarry

From 2003 to 2017, hundreds of kids and their families participated in digs at the
quarry through the Children's Museum of Indianapolis. That museum now houses
thousands of fossils from the Ruth Mason Quarry—primarily *Edmontosaurus* specimens as
well as *Triceratops*, *Tyrannosaurus rex*, and others.

To Read More About Ruth Mason, Dinosaurs, and Paleontologists

Black, Riley. "The Many Ways Women Get Left Out of Paleontology." *Smithsonian Magazine*,
June 7, 2018. https://www.smithsonianmag.com/science-nature/many-ways-women-get
-left-out-paleontology-180969239/.

Burnie, David. *The Kingfisher Illustrated Dinosaur Encyclopedia*. New York: Kingfisher, 2001.

Evans, Dallas C. "The Children's Museum of Indianapolis: A History of Leveraging Field
Expeditions and Lab Work to Enhance Public Engagement." In *Museums at the Forefront
of the History and Philosophy of Geology: History Made, History in the Making*, edited by
Gary D. Rosenberg and Renee M. Clary, 273–88. GSA Special Paper 535. Boulder, CO:
Geological Society of America, 2018. https://doi.org/10.1130/2018.2535(18).

Faith Country Heritage 1910–1985. Faith, SD: Faith Historical Committee, 1985.

Larson, Peter, and Kristin Donnan. *Bones Rock! Everything You Need to Know to Be a
Paleontologist*. Montpelier, VT: Invisible Cities Press, 2004.

Larson, Peter, and Kristin Donnan. *Rex Appeal: The Amazing Story of Sue, the Dinosaur That
Changed Science, the Law, and My Life*. Montpelier, VT: Invisible Cities Press, 2002.

Norton, O. Richard. "Bone Diggers from Hill City, South Dakota." *American West:
Travel & Life*, June 1989.

Acknowledgments

A special thanks to Gnene Fordyce for showing me Ruth's land and home
while sharing invaluable family history. I am also grateful to Rick Brooks,
Pete Larson, Dallas Evans, Darrin Pagnac, Randall Irmis, and Caroline
Buttler for helping me recreate the past.